RIGHTS FOR ANIMALS?

DEIRDRE ROCHFORD

FRANKLIN WATTS
NEW YORK • LONDON • SYDNEY

Revised edition 2000

First published in 1996 by
Franklin Watts
96 Leonard Street,
London EC2A 4XD

Franklin Watts Australia
14 Mars Road
Lane Cove
NSW 2066

© Franklin Watts 1996, 2000

Editor: Sarah Snashall
Series editor: Rachel Cooke
Designer: Nigel Soper, Millions Design

A CIP catalogue record for this book
is available from the British Library.

ISBN 0 7496 2414 0 (Hbk)
       0 7496 3781 1(Pbk)

Dewey Classification 179

Printed in Malaysia

Picture credits:
b=bottom, t=top, r=right, l=left:
The Body Shop: 15b; *The Bridgeman Art
Library*: p.4, 5t, 7b; *Bruce Coleman*: Dr
Inigo Everson p.7t, 13b; Hans Reinhard
p.17l; Stephen J Krasemann p.20bl; Erwin
and Peggy Bauer 20br; George McCarthy
p.21b; Norman Myers p.22b; John Shaw
p.23b; 27b; Jane Burton p.28t; Dr Eckart
Pott p.29t; *Environmental Picture Library*:
Pete Addis cover and p.10t; Mike Jackson
p.14; 17r; Stephen Whitehorne p.20t; Paul
Glendell p.26r; Andrew Testa p.27t;
Eye Ubiquitous: 10b; Paul Prestidge p.11;
Robert Harding: pp. 13t, 28b; Adam
Woolfitt pp. 6b, 19t; Hugh Routledge p.18t;
Shona Wood p.18b; *The Hutchison Library*:
Jesco von Puttkamer p.6t; Jeremy A
Horner p.9t; David Cuverd p.16b; Edward
Parker p.29b; *Panos Pictures*: 5b, 15t; Eric
Miller 23r; Betty Press 22r; *RSPCA*: 9b,
16t, 25(both); Alban Donohoe 8l; Wayne
Gray 24t; Nigel Rolstone 21t; *Rex Features*:
12l; *Today*: p.19b; Jenson p.26l; *Frank
Spooner*: 12r; *Trip/T Fisher*: 24b; *Zefa*: 8r

*Quotation credits (given from the top
of a page beginning with the left-
hand column):*
p.4 1 Stephen Budiansky, *Covenant of
the Wild: Why Animals Chose
Domesticity*, 1994; 2 Genesis 1:28,
The Bible
p.5 1 Lynne Truss, *The Times*, 1993; 2
Tom Regan, *The Case for Animal
Rights*, 1983; 3 American Society for
the Prevention of Cruelty to Animals,
spokesman, 1995
p.6 1 Harvey A Feit, McMaster
University, Canada, 1995; 2 Sarah
Dunant, *The Trouble With Animals*,
BBC TV, 1995; 3 David Street, *Fishing
in Wild Places*, 1989
p.7 1 Dan and Karen Trotter, *Woman's
Hour*, BBC Radio 4, 1995; 2 Andrew
Ottaway, a whale conservationist,
1995; 3 World Wide Fund for
Nature, 1996
p.8 1 Compassion in World Farming,
1995; 2 Delia Smith, *Complete
Cookery Course*, 1978
p.9 Michael Kefler, Chief Executive,
National Council of Shechita
Boards, 1996
p.10 The Vegetarian Society, 1995
p.11 1 Carla Lane, writer of TV
programmes *Butterflies* and *Bread*; 2
Alan Owen, small part-time farmer,
Private Eye, 6 October, 1995
p.12 1 Chief Seattle of the Suquamish
tribe in a letter to the President of the
United States, 1855; 2 People for the
Ethical Treatment of Animals campaign,
USA, 1980s; 3 *Trapper and Predator
Caller* magazine, USA, 1989
p.13 1 *The Facts About Fur*, Fur
Education Council, 1995
p.14 1 *New York Times* advertisement,
1980; 2 Charles Darwin, naturalist,
(1809-82)
p.15 1 British Association for the
Advancement of Science, 1990; 2
British Union for the Abolition of
Vivisection, 1995; 3 Andrew N Rowan
and Franklin M Loew, *The Animal
Research Controversy*, Tufts University
School of Veterinary Medicine,
USA, 1995
p.16 1 Jessica Szymczyk, Newsweek
1995; 2 Michael Robinson,
zoologist, 1994

p.17 1 John Bryant, *Fettered
Kingdoms*; 2 The Guide Dogs for the
Blind Association advertisement,
1995; 3 Robin Page, presenter of *One
Man and His Dog*, BBC TV, 1995
p.18 1 David Nicholson, UK racehorse
trainer, *The Duke*, 1995; 2 Action
Against the Grand National; 3 Richard
Pitman, *Turf Accounts, a
Connoisseur's Racing Anthology*,
Gollancz Witherby, 1995
p.19 People for the Ethical Treatment
of Animals, *Greyhound Racing: Death
in the Fast Lane*
p.20 1 Charles Dickens, novelist,
(1812-70); 2 Ronald van der Giesen,
director of information,
Natuurmomumenten, Holland, 1993;
3 The League Against Cruel Sports,
Foxes and Foxhunting, 1995; 4
Cameron Evans, secretary, Hunt
Saboteurs Association
p.21 2 David Bellamy, conservationist, 1993;
p.22 Care for the Wild News, 1995
p.23 1 Michael Kock, Zimbabwean
National Parks vet, 1993; 2 Greg
Neale, *Sunday Telegraph* newspaper,
1993; 3 *LifeWatch* magazine, 1995
p.24 1 London Zoo, 1995; 2 Brian
Davies, founder of the International
Fund for Animal Welfare
p.25 1 Julie Allday, RSPCA, 1995; 2 M
J G Bowman, *Connecticut Journal of
International Law*, USA, 1989; 3 The
American Society for the Prevention
of Cruelty to Animals, 1995
p.26 1 M Leepson, Congressional
Quarterly, USA, 1991; 2 from statements signed by the animal rights
group The Justice Department issued
through the Animal Liberation Front
Press Office, 1994
p.27 1 Michael Sissons, *The
Spectator*, 2 September, 1995; 2
American Society for the Prevention
of Cruelty to Animals, 1995
p.28 1 George Orwell, *Animal Farm*,
1945; 2 Melanie Phillips, *The Trouble
with Animals*, BBC TV, 1995; 3
Buddha, 566- 486BC
p.29 1 Bertrand Russell, philosopher,
(1872-1970); 2 Tom Regan, author of
The Case for Animal Rights, 1983.

Contents

King of the beasts?

" For two million years we were hunters; for ten thousand years we were farmers; for the last one hundred years we have been trying to deny it all… " Stephen Budiansky, *Covenant of the Wild: Why Animals Chose Domesticity*

The great changes of the past two centuries – industrialization, population growth and scientific and technological advancement – have completely transformed mankind's relationship with the animal kingdom. It is a development that many people have become increasingly concerned about.

Traditional thinking, influenced by religion, put animals firmly under mankind's power ('dominion').

" Then God said Let us make man in our image … and let him have dominion over the fish of the sea and over the birds of the air, and over the cattle … and over every creeping thing that creeps upon the earth… " Genesis 1:28, *The Bible*

Charles Darwin's revolutionary books *On the Origin of Species* (1859) and *The Descent of Man* (1871) challenged this view. By claiming that humans evolved from the apes, through natural selection, Darwin made nonsense of the idea that humans were set apart from the rest of the animal kingdom. His ideas sparked off the kind of furious debate that people have about animal rights today.

▼ *A lost ideal? In Christianity's Garden of Eden, all creatures lived together in harmony but with humans definitely superior to animals.*

animals do have the same rights as humans and that it is 'speciesism', a prejudice like racism or sexism, to think that we are more valuable than any animal.

66 *(If) it is wrong to treat weaker human beings, especially those who are lacking in normal human intelligence, as tools … or commodities, then it cannot be right, therefore, to treat animals as tools … and the like.* 99 *Tom Regan, The Case for Animal Rights*

Others argue that rights are unique to humans because only humans have free will, the ability to reason and make choices. Some people feel that it is wrong to talk of animal rights in a world where many people do not yet have basic rights.

However, most people can agree that animal rights should extend as far as to protect animals from unnecessary cruelty.

66 *We're not an animal rights organization. Animal rights is a loaded term in the US. We're a humane animal protection organization, lobbying for better treatment for animals.* 99 *American Society for the Prevention of Cruelty to Animals*

The theory behind animal rights is only a starting point. The issues become far more complicated when applied to the practical realities of the modern world. This book explores some of these issues and their implications for the animal rights debate.

▼ *The modern world is over-crowded and heavily industrialized. Humans have such dominance in the world that there can be no 'natural' balance now between mankind and animals.*

▲ *Darwin's theory that we are descended from apes was ridiculed by many people at the time but is now a generally accepted principle.*

66 *'Fish have rights' I read. Of course I laughed out loud. Rights to what? Fair trial? Freedom of expression? Abortion on demand?* 99 *Lynne Truss, journalist*

What are 'animal rights'? The usual explanation of 'rights' is a just claim to be treated a certain way by society, and to enjoy the benefits of that society. We must decide whether animals just have the right to be respected and treated kindly, or whether they have exactly the same rights as humans.

Some philosophers believe that

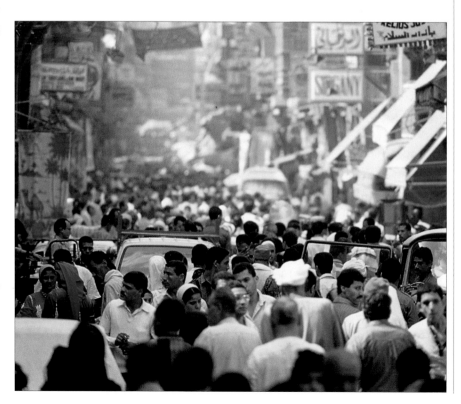

A natural resource?

Some people still live in the way that our forefathers did, hunting and scratching a living from the land. Unlike most of the modern world, their relationship with animals has remained unchanged by the advances of the 20th and 21st century.

❝ The Cree Indians have built their whole culture on killing. The irony is they have no problem accepting their equality with animals. ❞
Harvey A Feit, McMaster University, Canada

▲ *People campaign to preserve the threatened lifestyles of native people. These lifestyles are sometimes seen to embody the former healthy relationship between man and beast.*

The James Bay Cree Indians trapped animals for centuries. Their living was dependent on the prices fur fetched. When the Western world turned against the fur trade, their way of life collapsed. The Inuits were affected by the anti-sealing campaign in the same way.

❝ Only now are they beginning to recover from the effects. In their case, animal rights meant the loss of human ones. ❞ The Trouble With Animals, BBC TV

People with traditional lifestyles are often envied for their 'pure' lives

◀ *The sea turns red during the Grindadrap whale hunt. Such scenes horrify, but can they be justified by our need for whale products?*

▶ *It was once thought that the fish stocks would never dry up – now it looks like they may well do.*

which are close to nature. Yet, at the same time, modern society has turned against hunting peoples. It is hard to see where a respect for tradition becomes a toleration of cruelty.

❝ *Some men stood in the boats and thrust their spears into the whales. Some men were even trying to ride the whales into the shore. The waters rapidly began to turn crimson.* ❞
David Street, describing the Grindadrap, the Faroe Islanders' whale hunt, Fishing in Wild Places

The violent nature of the Faroese whale hunt disgusts many people. But the Faroese defend their right to hunt whales. They say that they depend on the sea, and everything in it, for their living.

❝ *The Faroese really do live with their environment and take a sustainable harvest of pilot whales. The argument has to be made in favour of traditional hunts.* ❞
Dan and Karen Trotter, Faroese islanders

The debate against these hunting peoples is not just about violence but is also about where the line is drawn between harvesting nature's sustainable resources and depleting them for profit. The whaling nations argue that there are enough whales to support their industry. The anti-whaling lobby argue that commercial whaling in any form would end with the extinction of all whales. Each side has a different set of statistics to support their argument.

❝ *I'm very depressed about it. In a way the conservationists have been guilty of hyping their own success. People think the whaling issue is clear-cut when it could yet be lost.* ❞
Andrew Ottaway, a whale conservationist

The anti-whaling lobby have one big advantage in the debate: whales are huge intelligent animals and people feel very emotional about their plight. Fish do not inspire the same emotion but overfishing has also become a problem. The extent of commercial fishing means that the world's fish stocks are disappearing fast.

❝ *Unless steps are taken to control the overfishing of the North Sea, we estimate favourites like cod and haddock will become extinct.* ❞
World Wide Fund for Nature

Demand for fish is now so great that it cannot be met through a sustainable harvest of fish. Increased fish farming may now be necessary to protect the falling wild stocks.

▶ *The saying 'dead as a dodo' reminds us of the dangers of extinction. These extraordinary birds were wiped out by 1800. One of the causes of their extinction was over hunting by humans.*

Is farming cruel?

How do farmed animals fare in today's world? The furious protests over live calf exports from the UK in 1995 took the rest of the world by surprise and put the spotlight onto the issue of farm animals' welfare.

❝In the UK, the rest of the European Union and beyond, hundreds of millions of farm animals are being kept in conditions which deprive them of even basic behavioural needs. ❞
Compassion in World Farming

Modern farming methods have been developed to deal with the huge demand for animal produce. In the US, 8 billion farm animals are killed for food each year, of which 7.2 billion are broiler chickens. In the UK, some 19 million sheep and lambs, 14 million pigs, 3.3 million cattle and 600 million broiler chickens are slaughtered for food each year. The farming community is pressurized by consumers to produce huge quantities of food at low prices.

❝Once upon a time chicken was a luxury. It is a credit to our farmers that they have put chicken within the reach of everyone at what, in these days, is a very reasonable price. ❞
Delia Smith, cookery writer

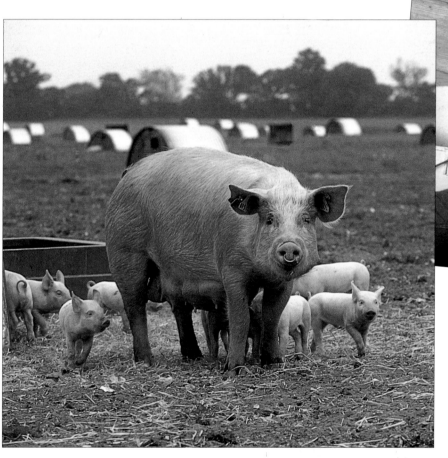

▲ This goose is being force-fed to expand its liver to make pâté de foie gras. Are animals paying the price for our luxury food?

◀ The pigs at this 'Freedom Foods' approved farm are treated humanely. Such farms are good for animals but may well be bad for food prices.

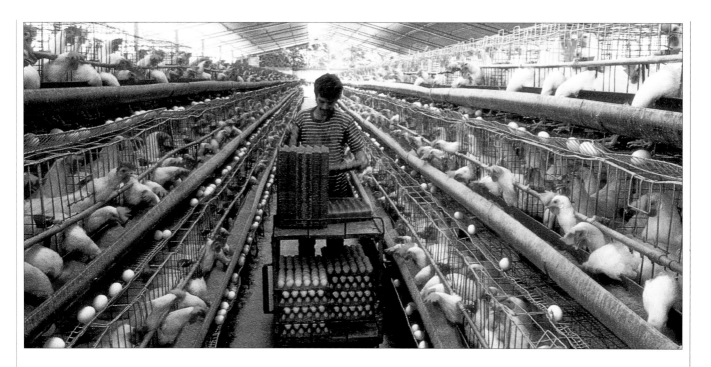

▲ *Battery hens are often packed in cages where they cannot stretch their wings, but these farms respond to the huge demand for eggs and chicken.*

With pressure on farmers from consumers, it is perhaps not surprising that farm animals are sometimes treated more like manufactured products than living creatures.

But intensive farming leads to a variety of problems: keeping animals indoors can lead to lameness and mastitis (sore udders) in dairy cattle and bone fractures for caged hens; the use of superovulation to produce multiple births in cattle can lead to problems at delivery.

Even farming methods which seem natural can bring problems. Pigs kept outside face foxes taking piglets, sunburn, and even drowning.

Religious practices raise a different kind of problem. In many countries, animals are legally required to be stunned with an electric shock before they are slaughtered. To do so goes against the beliefs of Muslims and Jews, which require that animals killed under Halal (Muslim) or Shechita (Jewish) procedures should not be stunned first. Religious and cultural ways should be respected, but are animals suffering for our beliefs?

66 *There is scientific evidence showing that shechita is as humane as any other slaughter technique.* 99 *National Council of Shechita Boards*

Farming welfare standards and expectations differ throughout the world. This, too, can cause problems. In Denmark in the early 1980s when conditions were improved for hens, eggs produced in worse systems were then imported because they were cheaper. In the UK, public opinion has turned against transporting animals for long distances, only to be slaughtered at the end. But the French public still want their meat fresh, which means transporting animals live. Perhaps the answer is a world where no one eats meat.

▼ *Veal calves are sometimes raised in restricting veal crates and fed on an exclusive milk diet. They are also exported live and the long journeys overseas are thought to be very stressful.*

Should we eat meat?

The average person in the West will consume 760 chickens, 29 sheep and 20 pigs in their lifetime. But if meat is not strictly necessary for our survival, why eat it?

66 *Most people become vegetarian because they believe it is wrong to slaughter animals for food.* 99
The Vegetarian Society

By 1999, 5 per cent of Britons were vegetarian. The American Vegetarian Resource Group reckons that between 0.3 and 1 per cent of Americans are true vegetarians. Young people in particular are becoming vegetarian.

Myths that vegetarianism is unhealthy have been shown to be untrue. Research on heart disease and cancer suggests that a vegetarian diet may even be healthier. However, others say that a vegetarian lifestyle goes against our omnivorous nature.

Some people are turning away from meat because they are worried about the quality of meat produced in modern intensive farming systems. Between 1996 and 1999, British beef was removed from sale around the world because of fears that meat carrying 'mad cow disease' (BSE) might infect humans. British cows became infected with BSE after controls on cattle feed were relaxed. Several Britons died of a brain disease similar to BSE.

▲ The traditional Western meal of 'meat and two veg' seems to be disappearing as more people lose their taste for red meat.

▲ Fish is acceptable to some who follow a vegetarian lifestyle.

Vegetarians do not eat meat, poultry, game or fish. Nor do they eat slaughter by-products, although sometimes these are less easily spotted. For instance, gelatin, which comes from animal bones, is used in ice cream, sweets and dairy products. Animal fats may be present in biscuits, cakes and margarines. Cheese, unless specifically vegetarian, is usually made with rennet, which is taken from calves' stomach lining. The real stumbling block for many vegetarians, though, is milk.

66 *It's no good crying out against the (calf export) trade if you are going to have milk.* **99** *Carla Lane, writer and animal welfare campaigner*

The only truly vegetarian way of life is vegan (eating no animal or dairy products), but this is difficult and possibly unhealthy. Many people feel that a less strict form of vegetarianism – perhaps, for example, still eating fish and dairy products – is acceptable and a worthwhile reduction in the consumption of animal products.

Some people think breeding animals for meat is an inefficient way to feed the world when 11 million children die of hunger each year. For every 10kg of grain fed to animals, only 1kg is converted to meat. On average, a meat eater's diet uses twice as much land as a vegetarian's, and good land is scarce throughout the world.

A world devoted to growing grain and vegetables would cause problems, too: the goodness in soils could quickly be used up by intensive farming; chemical fertilizers can be damaging to the environment. The best organic alternative to fertilizers is animal manure from keeping animals inside over the winter:

66 *I am at a loss to see how vegetarians would maintain their food supplies without the millions of tons of shit produced by the overwintering of beasts.* **99** *Alan Owen, part-time farmer*

And no-one can control the weather. Droughts in 1995 caused the worst world wheat harvest in 20 years and serious grain shortages in many countries. It seems that it is not yet possible for the world to be vegan.

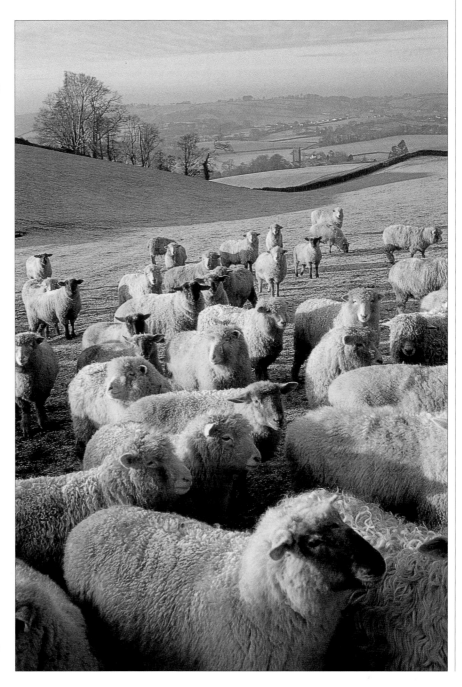

▼ *Many areas of rural beauty throughout the world are a result of the tradition of farming animals. What would happen to these areas if the whole world became vegetarian?*

Vanity, all is vanity?

Some people who do not eat meat also refuse to wear leather. Others won't eat meat, but do wear leather. This could be called hypocritical. If you are going to kill an animal for food, isn't it better to use every last scrap of it? The native American Indians believed this. They were horrified that the incoming settlers killed the buffalo herds for their skin alone.

“*I have seen a thousand rotting buffaloes on the prairie, left by the white man.* ” *Chief Seattle of the Suquamish tribe in a letter to the President of the United States, 1855*

The wearing of fur and other exotic animal skins such as crocodile has become a controversial issue. These animals are only killed for their skin. The more exotic the animal the more valuable their skin.

“*I'd rather go naked than wear fur* ” *People for the Ethical Treatment of Animals campaign*

◀ *Dressed to thrill or dressed to kill? The fur trade was rocked by powerful advertising campaigns started by those protesting against the fur trade.*

The anti-fur campaign shook the traditional fur markets. In the US, sales fell from nearly $2 billion per year in 1987 to a mere $500 million by 1999.

“*The European market fell in less than three years from the top consuming region to an area where furs are now looked upon with distaste.* ” *Trapper and Predator Caller magazine, USA*

Fur has became socially unacceptable to a large extent in the UK, but walk down a street in Milan and you will pass dozens of people in fur coats. New markets for fur have appeared – Hong Kong, Korea, China and the former Eastern Germany.

▼ *Russia is one of the countries where a fur coat is still a status symbol.*

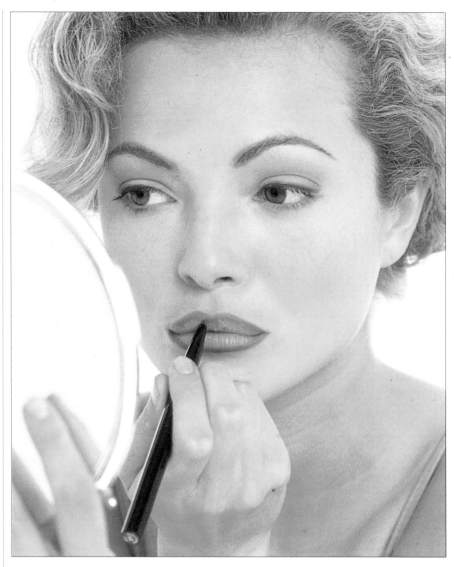

eyes, mouth and hair, from suntan cream to perfume – are often made from animal products. It could be argued that these products are not essential, but demand for them suggests that people feel otherwise. Cosmetic departments are usually right at the heart of a store, and a whole new industry has grown up around cosmetics for men.

The production of cosmetics without animal ingredients has become a huge industry. Unfortunately, that does not solve the problem because the law requires that all new ingredients in cosmetics must be tested on animals.

Can pain to animals be justified if it causes people to be out of pain?

◀ *Make-up and other cosmetics often contain ingredients that come from animals. Lanolin, a common ingredient, comes from sheep's wool.*

▼ *Until recently, many cosmetics and perfumes contained ingredients which came from whales. Now people want to protect whales and substitute ingredients are being used.*

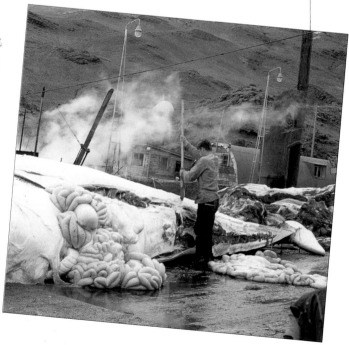

If the demand for fur continues, perhaps fur farming is a more acceptable way to meet that demand than trapping animals in the wild. Most pelts (fur skins) come from fur farms now. Fur was originally worn for practical reasons – warmth – but with alternatives available, surely it is just vanity to wear it now?

66 *Wearing fur can be just as easily justified as wearing leather, or eating eggs, meat, cheese and fish.* 99
Fur Education Council

One of the alternatives to fur is wool. But even wool is not free from debate. It does not involve killing any animals, but shearing is stressful for sheep and they would not shed their whole fleece in the wild.

Clothes are essential, but we 'wear' animals in different ways. Cosmetics – which includes anything we put on our skin,

Kill or cure?

Vivisection is one of the most fiercely argued aspects of the animal rights debate. Advertisements such as the one above have raised public awareness of the vivisection issue and businesses and governments have had to respond accordingly.

Revlon no longer test their products on animals and Britain banned cosmetics tests in 1998, after the European Council of Ministers blocked a proposed Europe-wide ban. The British law only stopped cosmetics experiments, not safety tests for household products such as food and toys. In the UK, 1.3 million animals are still used in such tests each year. In 1999, activists shut down a farm breeding cats for medical tests in a long siege which saw 350 arrests and cost the police £2.8 million.

The law demands that all new ingredients of any product must be tested to make sure that they are safe. Many of these tests have to be carried out on animals. These tests protect people from harmful products but at the expense of animal discomfort and often death.

Vivisection is also used in the progress of medicine.

I have all my life been a strong advocate for humanity to animals, and have done what I could in my writings to enforce this duty. I know that physiology cannot progress except by means of experiments on living animals, and I feel the deepest conviction that he who retards the progress of physiology commits a crime against mankind.
Charles Darwin, 19th-century naturalist

Anyone who has suffered from the following will have been treated by medicine developed as a result of research on animals: diabetes, asthma, cancer, polio, high blood pressure, kidney transplant, heart transplant and hip replacement.

◀ *Animal experimentation was necessary for the development of this child's asthma inhaler. Is his life more important than the lives of those animals who died?*

▶ It makes us uncomfortable to see pictures of experiments on animals, but are such experiments necessary evils for the progress of medicine?

Modern surgery and life-support systems for premature babies were also developed through experiments on animals.

The British Association for the Advancement of Science states:

❝ *Continued research involving animals is essential for the conquest of many unsolved medical problems such as cancer, AIDS and genetic, developmental, neurological and psychiatric conditions.* ❞
British Association for the Advancement of Science

But not everyone believes that animal research has contributed to the advancement of medicine:

❝ *Today we are losing the battle against diseases such as cancer, heart disease and AIDS, as millions of pounds are invested in misleading animal studies.* ❞ *British Union for the Abolition of Vivisection*

People are trying to develop alternatives to experiments on animals. Computer models can now be used in research, and living cells can be grown in 'culture', for use in tests. The problem is that these methods have to be validated – shown to work reliably in different laboratories – and this takes time.

Some scientists do not think that any of these methods is enough on its own and that it is still necessary to look at what is happening in the whole living animal.

❝ *The national trend in the United States is toward the reduced use of animals in biomedical research, but there is little chance of completely replacing animals.* ❞ *Tufts University School of Veterinary Medicine, USA*

How can we balance the need to relieve human suffering with the need to protect animals from unnecessary suffering?

◀ Almost all cosmetic ingredients have been tested on animals at some stage in the past. However, companies like 'The Body Shop', who have built their reputation on being animal friendly, do not test any of their finished products or raw ingredients on animals.

Man's best friend?

❝_I've been a vegetarian since I was 13. I don't wear cosmetics. I won't buy or wear fur. I refuse to wear or use leather. And I absolutely love animals. I get angry when I hear the terrible things animal-rights groups say about how we supposedly treat laboratory animals._**❞**
Jessica Szymczyk

Jessica Szymczyk looks after the animals in a research laboratory in the United States. She thinks they are often better cared for than many pets, or 'companion animals'. In the UK, the Royal Society for the Prevention of Cruelty to Animals

▼ _Dogs make loving companions, they can provide comfort and can reduce stress levels in people. But some people ask 'What is in it for the dog?' and want to see fewer pets._

(RSPCA) is very concerned about the number of mistreated and abandoned pets. They have tried to increase awareness about the cost and responsibility of owning a pet 'for life, and not just for Christmas', as one of their campaigns has put it.

There are 6.65 million pet dogs, 7.18 million cats, 1.42 million

budgerigars and 24.38 million fish in the UK alone. Pets are now a big business worldwide:

❝ _What we in the United States spend on our dogs and cats amounts to a sum greater than the entire economy of medieval Europe._ **❞**
Michael Robinson, zoologist

▲ _The RSPCA in the UK receives a phone call every 26 seconds. Neglect is still their worst problem._

Pet owners say that their animals are cherished companions, enjoying a better life than their wild cousins. It is a two way bond, providing nourishment for both sides. Hospitals have taken this idea

◀ ▲ Sheepdogs and guide dogs for the blind provide a worthy service to people. They are trained to go against their nature but are often well cared for in return. Are they exploited by people or is the relationship mutually beneficial?

dogs and studying the effects of stress on working dogs. Guide dogs work hard. Their role is particularly difficult, since they have to be trained to go against their natural instincts. This is true of any animal trained to work for humans, but some people believe that animals actually enjoy work.

❝ *I have long admired sheepdogs… The bond between man and dog is wonderful to see. It is based on trust, dedication and skill. The natural hunting instinct of the dog has been modified to herd… The dogs love and need work; the shepherds depend on the dogs and it is a system of two way reliance.* ❞
One Man and His Dog, BBC TV

Animals used in these ways are providing invaluable service to people. Using animals for entertainment may be more difficult to justify.

further, by bringing in dogs to visit patients. Research has shown that stroking a dog can help reduce people's blood pressure. Some people think that we should not keep pets at all.

❝ *I have not the slightest hesitation in saying that pet animals should be phased out of existence. My reason for this view is that pet animals are slaves and prisoners.* ❞
John Bryant, Fettered Kingdoms

If pets can be seen as slaves, what about working animals? Their contribution to our lives can be huge.

❝ *'Sit. - Stay. - Down. - Make an omelette.' The things we can't teach a dog to do, we teach the owner.* ❞
The Guide Dogs for the Blind Association advertisement

Providing dogs to act as people's eyes is only part of the work of Guide Dogs for the Blind. Other projects include solving sight problems in

A good sport?

In the developed world few animals are still used as working animals. However, many sports involving animals have developed from our working relationship with them.

Sport involves animals in different ways. Riding is one of the most popular sports, even if the child riding a pony on a trail seems a long way from the winner of the Grand National or Kentucky Derby. It is arguable which has the harder life, a riding school horse or a racehorse.

❝ *A racehorse is one of the most loved, and best looked after, of all animals.* **❞** *David Nicholson, racehorse trainer*

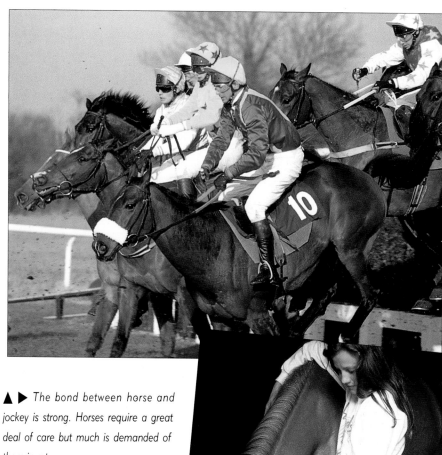

▲ ▶ *The bond between horse and jockey is strong. Horses require a great deal of care but much is demanded of them in return.*

Running, for horses, is a response to danger. In the wild they go round obstacles rather than jump them. So perhaps it is unnatural and stressful to expect them to take part in show-jumping, eventing, rodeo, polo, dressage or racing. This is the view of those groups that campaign against horse racing.

❝ *Racing is cruel and degrading to horses.* **❞** *Action Against the Grand National*

Either horses and other animals perform because they are too scared not to – or because they want to. Those who work with animals say that training and performance come down to mutual trust between horse and rider.

❝ *What many regular race-goers fail to understand is the bond between horse and rider. The whole thing revolves around confidence from the saddle being transmitted to the horse.* **❞** *Richard Pitman, A Connoisseur's Racing Anthology*

But are people really interested in the animals in the race or the money to be made from it? Racing (including betting and breeding) is the sixth largest industry in the UK. A great deal of money is made from animal sports all around the world.

66 *The natural speed and grace of greyhounds has been exploited for human benefit since the days of the Ancient Egyptians… Modern dog racing has turned this … breed into a mere commodity for greyhound breeders and racetrack owners. Greyhound racing is … big business. $3 billion was wagered on dog races in the United States in 1986, and that was at only 47 tracks in 14 states.* 99 *People for the Ethical Treatment of Animals*

A lot of money is riding on sport, with television deals, sponsors and advertising. Animal bodies and those involved in sport are co-operating more than they used to to ensure that animals do not suffer through being pushed too hard.

▶ *Gambling on animal sports is a huge business.*

▼ *Are some animal sports more acceptable than others? Some people think that bull fighting is barbaric. Others see it as part of their lives and culture.*

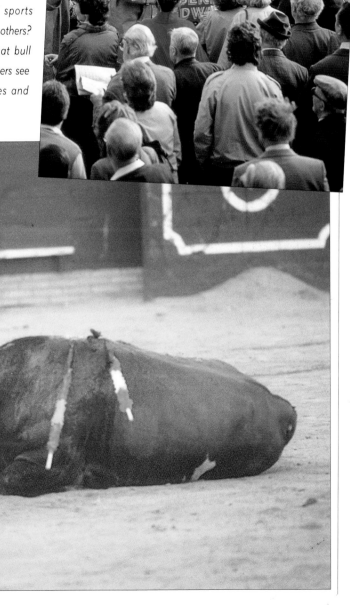

A right to hunt?

Famous horse races like the Grand National developed from fox-hunting. People raced their hunt horses against their friends' for fun. Jump racing is still run under 'National Hunt' rules.

Although we still hunt in the sea, on an individual level we no longer depend on hunting for our food. However, hunting – whether birds, mammals, such as foxes and deer, or fish – continues as a sport. In the UK, 4 million people hunt, shoot and fish.

❝ There is a passion for hunting deeply implanted in the human breast. ❞ *Charles Dickens, 19th-century novelist*

Attitudes have changed since Dickens' day.

❝ *Hunting is not a natural thing [for humans].* ❞ *Ronald van der Giesen, director of information, Natuurmomumenten, Holland*

▼ *Hunters keep the stuffed heads or sometimes feet of the animals that they have killed as sporting trophies to show the variety and quantity of their kills. Some find this practice unpleasant.*

▲ *Fishing is seen as one of the most peaceful sports, but those against fishing say that it is painful and distressing for the fish.*

▼ *Some see hunting as a way of being part of the natural order of things, with man pitted against the wild. Others see hunting as a pointless destruction of beautiful animals.*

Others feel that some kinds of hunting are more deplorable than others. In the UK, the League Against Cruel Sports is committed to banning fox-hunting. But some members do not oppose sport-fishing even though research shows that fish feel pain.

Fox-hunting is banned in Germany and Holland and it has a vocal opposition in the UK.

66 Fox-hunting has the same purpose as the now illegal pastimes of dogfighting, bear baiting and cockfighting – to provide amusement for human beings. 99 The League Against Cruel Sports

Anti-hunt groups argue that banning fox-hunting would save the lives of foxes:

66 We have been in existence for almost 30 years, and in that time thousands of lives have been saved. 99 Hunt Saboteurs Association

Their view is challenged.

66 The abolition of fox-hunting will not make a hap'orth of difference to animal welfare. Well over 200,000 foxes are killed in the UK every year by much worse methods than fox-hunting. 99 Richard Course, former chairman of the League Against Cruel Sports, Horse & Hound magazine

Hunters argue that we live in a world where, for better or worse, animals are controlled, and that hunting is a more natural method than snaring, gassing or mangling animals under a car's wheels.

In the past few years, the

▲ ▶ *Fox hunting is disapproved of by many. Those who live and work in the countryside often believe that it is a more humane way of culling foxes than snaring or trapping.*

arguments have moved from cruelty on to environmental issues. It is argued that country sports bring money and jobs into rural parts. They have shaped the countryside as we know it and value it today, preserving small woods, ponds, and wild ground that would have gone under the plough otherwise.

66 Rural Britain is not a theme park which has to be kept nice for weekends, regardless of the cost during the week. We live in a human-made and human-maintained landscape. The habitats within which our wildlife lives is shaped and cared for by the skills of rural people. The life of the countryside is dependent upon the livelihoods of the people who live there, not the prejudices of those who don't. 99
Richard Burge, Chief Executive, Countryside Alliance

Throughout history, landowners' desire to hunt has provided areas of conserved beauty in the form of game parks. Blood sports have ironically preserved animal habitats. Hunting people were arguably the first conservationists.

66 Without the conservation management provided by country shooting, all this beautiful countryside and everything that it contains, the flowers, the wildlife and the songbirds would have disappeared a long time ago. 99
David Bellamy, conservationist

A battle for survival?

Some animals are being hunted to extinction. The debate over 'big game' hunting, particularly in Africa, is not just about the pain of the individual animal but about the survival of an entire species.

The discussion over the African elephant is an example of this debate. CITES (the Convention on International Trade in Endangered Species of Wild Fauna and Flora) lists the elephant on Appendix 1. This means that any trade in ivory, skin and meat is prohibited. Several south African countries want to downgrade the elephant to Appendix 2. This would allow them to do some trade in skin and meat.

For some, the argument is simple. These people believe that the elephant must have full protection from any type of trade. They believe that the ivory ban saved the elephants from being wiped out and that to start the trade again would be unthinkable. They argue that the culling (selective killing) of elephants must stop. They believe that elephants will encourage tourism.

❝ *There is an alternative to South Africa cruelly culling its extra elephants – realizing the potential for ecotourism.* **❞** *Care For The Wild*

Others argue that the elephant is not endangered. They believe that it is better to teach local people to

▲ *Richard Leakey, a conservationist, burned ivory in Kenya as a protest against poaching.*

▼ *Life in Africa can be hard for people and animals alike. A balance must be found that suits both.*

▶ *A black rhino has its horns removed by conservationists in Kenya to protect it from poachers. It is strange and sad that animals have to be mutilated to be protected.*

value the elephants as a potential crop, rather than a threat to their existing crops. Tourism alone, they argue, is too fragile to support the elephants. Developing countries should be allowed to use trade in elephants to bring in funds.

66 *The old preservationist philosophy is no longer working. Beyond tourism, animals have got to start paying their own way. We're protecting them into extinction.* 99 *Michael Kock, Zimbabwean National Parks vet*

South Africa has been reviled by conservationists throughout the world for its policy of culling elephants in areas where they say there are too many. In turn, President Nelson Mandela argues that South Africa may have found political freedom, but the country faces huge problems, and needs all the money it can raise – even if this is from elephants.

66 *Mandela: 'Let us eat elephants'.* 99 *Sunday Telegraph newspaper*

International legislation from CITES is sometimes ineffective. Perhaps the most notorious animal trade is the tiger industry. At the beginning of this century there were some 80,000 tigers in the wild, now

there are less than 5,000. Three species have disappeared since the 1950s.

66 *Across Asia the trade in tiger parts continues because of the Far Eastern traditional medicine culture. In 1990 a Taiwanese brewery imported 2,000kg of bones – more than 50 tigers – to support a yearly production of 100,000 bottles of tiger bone wine!* 99 *LifeWatch magazine*

The tiger is threatened by opposed human values ('We think our medicine works' versus 'We think your medicine methods are cruel'). How can we ensure that endangered species are fully protected? Perhaps the only way is to keep them away from humans, even if this means sacrificing their freedom in sanctuaries, reserves and zoos.

▼ *Ecotourism makes African animals profitable. This provides protection for animals and financial support for Africa.*

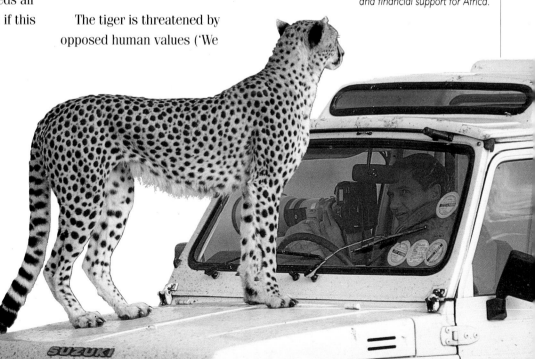

SUZUKI

How can we protect animals?

" In an ideal world, all living things would be able to live in their natural environment. However, this century we have seen the overpopulation of our planet by the human being and the struggle to survive has become virtually impossible for many other species. Captive breeding programmes in zoos are, for many kinds of animals, the only hope left of avoiding extinction. " London Zoo

There are 5,000 zoos around the world. These can offer protection to many species and help to boost populations in the wild. Moreover, zoos can be educational, giving people a chance to see live animals.

Some people feel, however, that zoos are an outdated concept and that their main purpose is our entertainment.

" Zoos, for many species, are a jail for life. At the end of the day, they just provide work for zookeepers. " Brian Davies, founder of the International Fund for Animal Welfare

Some people feel that zoos are a way of protecting animals, particularly those in danger of extinction. Animals can also be protected by using the law.

Animal welfare and animal rights

pressure groups have persuaded governments to pass laws about the treatment of animals. The world's first animal protection organization was the Royal Society for the Prevention of Cruelty to Animals (RSPCA), founded in 1824 in the UK. Now there are groups worldwide, from Colombia to Australia, Fiji to the Czech Republic.

Legal protection for animals varies hugely throughout the world. Switzerland has had a comprehensive law since 1978; the Spanish Parliament rejected a

▼ *This polar bear is a long way from its icy home. The zoo is an unnatural environment.*

▶ Zoos provide veterinary care for animals, as well as breeding stock for rare species.

national animal welfare law in 1992; Israel introduced its first Animal Protection Act in 1994. In the UK, animal laws cover cruelty, experiments, slaughter, exhibitions (performing animals or animals in film), animal establishments, birds, markets, transit, game laws and conservation.

66 Countries that do not have many humanitarian problems are more likely to have stronger animal protection laws. If a country is emerging from civil war, or having problems feeding its people, animal welfare comes way down the line. 99
RSPCA

As well as national legislation, animals in Europe are covered by laws of the European Parliament and Council. These laws mainly cover trade in animals. Conventions (formal meetings) have been set up to discuss the protection of animals. The Bonn Convention is concerned with migratory animals; the Washington Convention, better known as CITES, is concerned with international trade in animals.

Unfortunately, any law is only as effective as its enforcers. This is a particular problem with international laws where so many different countries are involved, each with different interests.

66 The present (international law) situation leaves much to be desired. Certainly, the need exists for a truly global instrument with effective enforcement procedures. 99
Connecticut Journal of International Law, USA

▲ *Richard Martin (who was responsible for the British anti-cruelty act of 1822) took Bill Burns to court for wounding his donkey.*

Speed can also be a problem with legislation:

66 It took 14 years to get a law prohibiting animal experimentation in elementary and high schools. 99 The American Society for the Prevention of Cruelty to Animals

Some people are dissatisfied with the law's ability to protect animals. Some people feel that violence is the only way to get things changed.

▶ *This photograph was used by the RSPCA in a poster campaign with the caption, 'The only thing that's protected in this photograph is the man's identity'. The law has been changed and foxes are now protected under British law.*

The end justifies the means?

Since 1977 there has been a rise in violence in the name of animal rights. Vandalism and bombs have caused millions of dollars' and pounds' worth of damage.

" On June 7 1990, Secretary Sullivan made headlines … by calling militant animal rights activists 'terrorists'. " *Congressional Quarterly, USA*

In March 1995, the London Metropolitan Police's Special Branch set up a new group to investigate 'animal rights terrorism'. Was this a recognition of a darker side of animal protest, or an over-reaction?

The FBI defines terrorism as 'the unlawful use of force or violence against persons or property to intimidate or coerce a government, the civilian population, or any segment thereof, in furtherance of political or social objectives.' The animal activists involved argue that radical, even extreme, measures are justified to protect animals who cannot speak, or act, to protect themselves.

" We never had faith in the political system so used direct action to fight the many obscenities inflicted on the animal kingdom. We anticipate more will join the war being fought by so many good people outside the hopelessness of asking people with nasty habits nicely to stop destroying animals' lives. They insult humanity so deserve to be insulted and humiliated. They deserve more we think, soon they'll get it… We only have to get lucky once. "

From statements signed by the animal rights group The Justice Department issued through the Animal Liberation Front Press Office

Victims of these 'terrorists' have included scientists, store-keepers, pub owners, farmers, children, pharmacists and Prince Charles. The case of Colin Blakemore, an Oxford scientist, is typical. The night before Christmas Eve, 1993, he received a letter bomb filled with needles. His daughters have been threatened with kidnapping and death.

▲ *This shop was set on fire by animal rights activists to protest against the selling of fur coats. They put human lives at risk in order to help save animals.*

◄ *The people who protested about the export of live animals were prepared to risk their own freedom and even their lives for animal rights.*

The number of people involved is very small (around 100 in the Animal Liberation Front in the USA claimed responsibility for about 60 per cent of incidents). But they make themselves known:

66 We can currently tune in on the Internet to a ten-page boast by the animal rights organization, the Justice Department. It lists some 150 people who have received potentially lethal missiles through the post. They are particularly proud of their latest weapon. It consists of a mouse-trap, welded to whose spring bar is a razor-blade coated with HIV-infected blood. 99 Spectator *magazine*

The vast majority of animal groups distance themselves from any violence:

66 We're a moderate, middle of the road organization. We would rather sit down at a table with people than throw paint at their doors. 99 American Society for the Prevention of Cruelty to Animals

Activists who go to violent lengths regard themselves as crusading for animals. All movements have their radical supporters; we have to decide at what point acceptable forceful protest becomes unacceptable. Can it ever be right in a country with democratic elections for a group of people to use violence to try to change what they see as wrong?

▲ Anti-hunt saboteurs interrupt a fox hunt by trying to stop the foxhounds chasing the fox. This puts the horses, their riders and the saboteurs in danger.

▲ The usual face of animal welfare groups is peaceful. Here, people queue to sign their protest in a streetside petition.

Rights for animals?

> *All animals are equal, but some are more equal than others.*
> George Orwell, *Animal Farm*

People's behaviour towards animals is inconsistent. In the West cows are killed for food and dogs are kept as companions. But people eat dogs in China. Many people who are opposed to experiments on animals would not be opposed to receiving medical treatment which had been developed through experiments on animals. Some people argue that humans are not superior to animals, whilst rejecting human animal behaviour in the form of hunting.

Some people feel that the animal rights debate obscures the human rights debate.

◀▲ It is much easier to feel emotional about a baby seal than rats on a rubbish heap, but logically they should be entitled to the same care and protection from people.

> *I don't see the same moral outrage shown over animals being exhibited on the part of suffering humanity.* The Trouble With Animals, BBC TV

> *When a man has compassion for all living creatures, only then is he noble.* Buddha

If we care about animals' suffering, then our first duty is to see that they do not suffer. But people seem unable to agree on whether some animal suffering can be justified or whether animals have the right never to suffer. If animals have rights, we have to agree what those are.

Some argue it would be impossible for animals to enjoy exactly the same rights that humans do:

66 *The logical extension of animal rights is votes for oysters.* 99 *Bertrand Russell, 20th-century philosopher*

Others say that we are just too unimaginative or frightened to go the whole way and give animals full rights. A radically new approach is needed:

66 *It is not larger, cleaner cages that are called for in the case of laboratory animals, but empty cages; not more traditional commercial farms, but no commerce in animal flesh, whatever… How we achieve these ends and whether we achieve these ends are largely political and educational questions.* 99 *Tom Regan, author of The Case for Animal Rights*

Rights come with responsibilities. Human rights have developed from deciding certain codes of acceptable behaviour. Would we expect animals to abide by our rules? Would we take a cat to court for killing a bird, or prosecute a dolphin for killing a porpoise? We also have to decide where 'life' begins and ends. If we

▶ *This bird has been caught in an oil slick. Since our world creates problems for animals, is it is our responsibility to look after them?*

give animals rights, maybe we should give plants and lower organisms the same consideration.

Perhaps arguing about 'rights' confuses the more immediate issue of animal suffering. A division has grown between people who believe in animal rights and those who believe in animal welfare. True animal rights supporters object to both animal suffering and killing. Animal welfare supporters object to animal suffering, but are prepared to accept animals are used by humans, whether for food, clothing, health, recreation or companionship. Animal welfare supporters believe that animals have a right to be treated with respect and compassion, but not to be treated the same way as humans.

Most people fall into what American philosopher Strachan Donnelly calls 'the troubled middle' on this. Where do you put yourself?

▼ *The natural world has its own laws: bears eat fish and fish eat flies. Where do humans fit in? Have our actions upset the natural order or merely changed it?*

Glossary

ANIMAL ACTIVISTS: People who take direct, and often militant action, in the name of animal rights.

ANIMAL WELFARE: Concern for animals' well-being and ensuring that they are not harmed or abused.

BATTERY HENS: Hens kept in stacks of cages in sheds and farmed intensively for their eggs.

BEHAVIOURAL NEEDS: The basic conditions required for an animal to behave naturally.

BROILER CHICKENS: Young birds reared for food production.

BSE: Bovine Spongiform Encephalopathy, known as 'mad cow disease'. BSE infected beef is thought by some people to be the cause of a similar brain disease in humans.

CULLING: Selective killing to remove the weakest/oldest animals to maintain stocks at a sustainable level.

ECOTOURISM: Tourism to places of ecological value. These are often areas of conservation.

ENDANGERED: Any species whose numbers are so reduced it is in danger of being wiped out.

EXTINCTION: The complete disappearance of a species for ever.

HALAL: Meat from animals that have been killed according to Muslim law.

HERBIVORE: An animal that feeds only on plants.

HUMANE: Compassionate (here towards animals); a humane killer is one that aims to kill an animal as painlessly as possible.

LOBBY: A group of people who try to influence law-makers on behalf of a particular interest.

NATURAL SELECTION: Process whereby the strongest of a species is seen to survive and breed the next generation, at the cost of weaker members.

OMNIVORE: An animal that feeds on both vegetable and animal foods.

OVERWINTERING: Keeping animals inside during the winter.

PELTS: The skins of fur-bearing animals, when they have been removed from those animals.

RENNET: Curdled milk found in the fourth stomach of a young calf, used for curdling milk to make cheese. It can also be made from the lining of the calf's fourth stomach.

SHECHITA: The Jewish method of killing animals for food.

SLAUGHTER BY-PRODUCTS: Material left over from slaughtered animals once the edible meat has been removed that is used to make other products.

SPECIESISM: A belief that animals are inferior to humans and can be used for human benefit without any regard to what they may suffer.

SUPEROVULATION: Artificially inducing a female animal to produce more eggs than is produced naturally.

SUSTAINABLE HARVEST: A harvest that takes only what is needed in terms of resources while ensuring that stocks are not exhausted.

TERRORISM: The deliberate use of violence and terror to achieve an end (usually political).

VEGAN: A person who will not eat or use any animal products.

VEGETARIAN: A person who doesn't eat meat or fish or any other animal products, but will eat dairy products.

VIVISECTION: The performance of experiments on living animals.

Useful Addresses

UK

British Union for the Abolition of Vivisection
16a Crane Road
London N7 8NN
Tel: 020 7700 4888

Compassion in World Farming
5a Charles Street
Petersfield
Hampshire GU32 3EH
Tel: 02380 264208

London Zoo
Regent's Park
London NW1 4RY
Tel: 020 7722 3333

League Against Cruel Sports
83-87 Union Street
London SE1 1SG
Tel: 020 7403 6155

Research Defence Society
58 Great Marlborough Street
London W1V 1DD
Tel: 020 7287 2818

Royal Society for the Prevention of Cruelty to Animals
(RSPCA)
The Causeway
Horsham
Sussex RH12 1HG
Tel: 08705 555999

World Wide Fund for Nature (UK)
Panda House, Weyside Park
Godalming
Surrey GU17 1XR
Tel: 01483 426444

Australia

RSPCA
201 Rookwood Road
Yagoona NSW 2199
Tel: 02 709 5433

Animal Welfare League
45 Herley Avenue
West Hoxton NSW 2171
Tel: 02 606 9333

Facts to think about

◆ Cosmetic tests on animals in Britain fell from 31,304 in 1980 to 1,319 in 1997, before being banned. In Europe, around 35,000 such tests were conducted in 1997.

◆ The proportion of Britons describing themselves as vegetarian rose from 2 per cent in 1984 to 5 per cent in 1999. In the same period, national meat consumption rose from 61kg to 72kg per person per year.

◆ The West Indian communities of St Vincent and the Grenadines are permitted by the International Whaling Commission to kill (strike) two Humpback whales each year.

◆ A National Opinion Poll for Animal Aid in 1998 found that only 60 per cent of British adults believe animals suffer at slaughter, compared to 76 per cent of 15–24 yrs olds.

◆ 12,000 specially-farmed cats and dogs were used in medical experiments in Britain in 1998. The same number are abandoned by UK pet owners every three days.

◆ Between 1996 and 1997, British farm incomes dropped by one half.

Between 1997 and 1998, they dropped by one half again.

◆ Over 2 million whales were killed in the last century. Once there were 250,000 blue whales in the southern oceans; today there may be fewer than 1,000.

◆ Jewish slaughterers, who receive nearly 7 years' training in kosher techniques, kill 2,488,000 animals a year in the UK. But only 17,176 of these animals are eaten as the rest are condemned when inspected through a number of religious laws.

Index